The Sales Mindset

JYOTENDRA THOKCHOM

CONTENTS

ACKNOWLEDGEMENTS

would like to thank my family, friends, colleagues (past and present), and clients who have taught me and counselled me. I thank them all for being kind, generous and patient with me. I have truly learned a lot from each of them and will always treasure my lessons.

I am especially indebted to my wife, Pratiksha, for her prayers, patience, kindness, and love, and for being there and supporting me through every mile and across every distance that I needed to cover as a sales leader. Her sacrifices and her strength have been pivotal in shaping my life.

ABOUT THE AUTHOR

Jyotendra was born in Imphal in the Indian state of Manipur. He grew up in Kurseong, Darjeeling, in the Himalayas, a district celebrated for its panoramic beauty and delicious Darjeeling tea.

Excelling in B2B sales, he rose from a call centre agent to become the regional vice president at a premier IT & business process outsourcing (BPO) company, leading international teams to manage and deliver IT and outsourced services to the biggest brands in the travel and hospitality industries. He has more than two decades of experience in account management, operations and sales, garnered within top tier IT solutions providers across India and the UK. He worked extensively in global markets including India, Asia, the Middle East, UK, Europe and North America.

In the autumn of 2018, Jyotendra left his employment to establish Digitek Consulting in United Kingdom. He works with C-suite professionals in BPO and IT Services, advising on and implementing global growth strategies. In his current capacity, he has also supported capability development, software product development, and call centre set up internationally.

PREFACE

Sales take a corporation from the dusty, windswept deserts of nowhere to the calm, air-conditioned, cocktails-and-caviar ambience of success. Without sales, Starbucks was just coffee, and an odd-looking mermaid.

Yet to other functions, and even the most senior leaders, what the sales team does, and how they do it, is something of a mystery. Their expenses are a lot higher than the guys in finance, that is for sure. But how do they land deals? And are they performing at their best? Let us hope so.

Our views are easily clouded by outdated ideas or less-than-favourable stereotypes. It is easy to imagine a huckster touting shortcuts and maxims. "Sell me this pen!" he cries, with a slightly desperate expression and a biro.

Forget the biro. And the desperation.

A high value, quality sale in a B2B environment is driven by strategy, values, and behaviours. Contracts – and therefore relationships – are long-term: a three, five, or even seven-year commitment may be required from the client in exchange for the delivery of complex projects or services. This is why strategy, values and behaviours are so important. And we can't just talk about them. We have to live them. But if it is midnight, and you are lying awake in the darkness, worrying about the survival of your business, these three things may feel like luxuries you cannot afford. Even if your business is trundling along acceptably, you may not be asking questions about strategy, values, or behaviours.

Instead, you ask the most natural and logical questions there are for any entrepreneur, leader, or sales professional. You ask:

- How do I get new clients?
- How do I maximise the value – the wallet share – of those clients?

For the most driven and focused entrepreneurs, these questions can act like panic-inducing roadblocks. Hunting for solutions, scouring the landscape for what you need, you may forget that the most valuable thing – your biggest asset – is already with you.

My biggest asset...My bank balance? That's not an asset. I'm in the overdraft. I have been all month.

I'm not talking about money (yet).

Is it...do you mean...property?

Your biggest asset is you, and your people – your team. But being hard-working, smart, creative, and having good intentions, on their own terms, is not enough for a business, and it is not enough for the sales team. This is where the strategy comes in.

Still, a strategy in place, all the hard work, brains, creativity, and good intentions will not be enough if the leadership's ambitions are not high enough. The values and behaviours of your team are apparent to every client and potential client, whether the team thinks about it or not. They are reflected in every interaction, and every process (or lack of). It is about so much more than handling a meeting, or even an objection.

Take the quarterly business review. Leading on projects, I did not leave the features of the day – topics, exchanges, location, what was served at lunch – to chance. I did not hope for the best, hope that fate might intervene, and in my favour. No – critical meetings with clients were tightly planned, I would say almost choreographed. I think of a film director on set, working with precision, care, and determination to create something wonderful. That is what I mean by ambition.

Make no mistake, this book is a practical, no-nonsense look at increasing sales, and maximising the value of clients, with real-life case studies, examples and anecdotes to illustrate points. I'm not asking different questions, only re-framing how we say them.

Yet strategy, values and behaviours are quite long, heavy words to carry around with us. I can imagine them packed into a large, camo print backpack, with thick straps around the shoulders, a pack that will weigh more with every passing mile. Why make things hard on ourselves? Let's make the pack lighter. Let's make those long, heavy words manageable. Let's call them *The Sales Mindset*.

Who this book is for

Although some learning has wider relevance, The Sales Mindset is focused on B2B sales, and particularly services – IT, software, customer service and BPO. The context is global – while India is a long-standing player in outsourcing, you will find competing services in the Philippines, South Africa, South American nations, Eastern Europe, North and Central Africa, the Caribbean, and many other places. In these environments, one expects evolving technology, new requirements, big projects and, very often, big personalities.

You may be a business owner or entrepreneur looking for growth. You may be an ambitious sales leader, or a sales team contributor. If you are, you will get a lot from this book. Alternatively, you may be a leader in another field, looking to learn more about how an optimised sales team thinks and works. You are about to find out.

How this book is structured

Read in full, The Sales Mindset offers an integrated perspective with a logical narrative flow. However, there is no need to go from first page to last in strict order to benefit from and enjoy the material. Each chapter is a self-contained look at a particular facet of B2B sales and, depending on your current position and goals, you may prefer to go straight to the chapters most relevant to you.

INTRODUCTION

"Why don't you just take the customer for dinner?"

The total contract value (TCV) in a three-year deal is easily more than $1m, and a TCV of $10m is not uncommon. A signature on the dotted line usually represents the agreement and advocacy of not just one stakeholder, but many, all with different goals and backgrounds. Yet, at a sticky point in negotiations or in delivery, a senior leader may turn to the sales team and ask, "Why don't you just take the customer for dinner?" Believe me, I have heard it.

The food may be good, but it is never that good. Time away from the office, in a new and pleasant setting, can help build relationships. But they can go to any restaurant they want without your invitation and swapping strip lighting for chandeliers does not remove the obstacles standing in the way of an agreement or quieten shouts if you have not delivered.

The persuasive power of a wine list is one of a few notions that is still colouring perceptions of the sales profession. These ideas look past the true requirements of an effective sales team, yet they are so popular, so persistent, and so often voiced, that despite being cliches, or misunderstandings, they have the staying power of myths.

Some myths deserve their longevity: the legends of Greek and Norse mythology, for example, still inform and inspire. Others do not. Let us squash the myths that do not help us.

Myth No. 1

"If you are in sales, you need to be thick-skinned."

In this story, the salesperson just keeps banging on the door. They heard a "No!" yelled through the letterbox an hour ago, but they won't give up, not until they get their sale.

Here, thick-skinned really means stubborn. But stubborn is the less admirable, and far less successful, cousin of determined. The determined salesperson seeks to understand the factors in play behind a yes or a no, the stubborn salesperson just won't go away.

Myth No. 2

"This salesperson can guarantee future sales."

A variation of this may be heard from the most eager, and perhaps most junior, salesperson who declares, promises, guarantees, "I will sell 12 cars in 12 months."

I hear that and I think they won't sell any! I cannot guarantee you a sale. I don't believe anyone who says they can.

Myth No. 3

"Salespeople talk a lot."

It is true I speak to many people, but my intention is to listen. Listen, and then assimilate what the customer has said. Talking a lot – a volley of words – is not a technique, and never a plan.

Myth No. 4

"Salespeople lie a lot."

The lies we are being warned about are likely to be promises that can't be kept – promises given to convince the customer and get the sale.

The foundation of this story is that the salesperson has an incentive to lie, but a lie, once uncovered, erodes trust, so it is especially dangerous when relationship-building and in contractual agreements. Lies are not part of a professional salesperson's toolkit.

It is possible that being stubborn, unusually talkative, or a little too relaxed about the facts may earn a few sales. But these methods are totally at odds with a concept central to long-term success: positioning.

What is positioning?

How fortunate the heroes of business lore were. To have the *first* toothpaste brand. The *first* bubble gum. The *first* washing machines and fridges. The *first* vacuum cleaners.

Being first with a product, in a market, or to achieve something, means you are visible in the way being second or third never will. The first man on the moon, Neil Armstrong, occupies a space in every schoolchild's mind, and if you are old enough to have seen the broadcast in July 1969, then that space is probably even bigger.

In sales and marketing, this consciousness, this space in someone's mind, is called positioning. (If you are looking for an in-depth look at positioning, I recommend the excellent *Positioning: The Battle for your Mind* by Al Ries and Jack Trout).

But being first in anything is increasingly rare. As an entrepreneur or sales leader, you are likely competing in a crowded market, alongside many others selling similar services and products.

You used to be able to compete on cost. But cost arbitrage is no longer enough to secure a client's loyalty, because there are many cost-effective options for them to choose from.

You want to be first in a client's mind, in the way Neil Armstrong is for anyone who ever looked at the moon, but you are not first on the moon. In fact, there are so many other suited-and-booted moon explorers, you are starting to wish a few of the others would just clear off.

When you meet a prospect or are in the first months of a new contract, you look much like all the others. The client is not conscious of you in a way that is going to increase the quality of conversations and sales opportunities: your positioning is weak.

To be a viable frontrunner in the competition for new deals, your positioning must be strong. Strong positioning means healthy, profitable, and enjoyable business. Achieving it requires a highly focused approach to sales strategy, sales process, and account management. Let's get started.

1

A STEP INTO SALES STRATEGY

The skies fell silent, high streets were deserted. It was March 2020, and one nation after another started declaring the strictest lockdowns – no travel, no eating out, no shopping, no exercise – as administrations worked to contain Covid-19. For most office workers, business relocated from a glass-panelled building to their home, and, possibly, a rickety kitchen table.

I saw organizational leaders seized by panic. But while the supermarket shelves lay empty, I could see that in B2B, transactions were still happening. A deadly pandemic could not stop business.

What can stop business? Fear. A lack of focus. A lack of strategic thinking.

An unforeseen event, like a pandemic, may require a business to reassess its sales strategy, and urgently: a new approach is necessary, and should be deployed quickly. Although a vastly different set of circumstances, the excitement and myriad possibilities of a new venture can prompt not dissimilar feelings: uncertainty, anxiety, even a kind of temporary intellectual paralysis.

If there is a void where an apt sales strategy should be, it may feel too early for charts and meetings. You may not feel ready for the critical analysis that detailed sales strategic planning requires. If this is you, there is just one thing you need to do...

Follow the money

Where is money changing hands? Seek out and absorb the relevant market intelligence, industry analytics and data-driven insights from reputable sources.

I can recommend TechCrunch, a news outlet dedicated to reporting on the tech industry, and with a special focus on start-ups. Bloomberg Businessweek is another high-quality news source to keep an eye on.

Money will always be changing hands somewhere, and activity levels do not always correlate with the most obvious, significant or even perilous economic conditions. Let us look at 2020, a year unquestionably burdened by the economic and social ramifications of a global pandemic, which left some sectors stricken, temporarily at least. Q1 reporting (MoneyTree™ Report, Q1 2020, CB Insights and PWC) showed a marked slowdown in US and global deal activity and funding, albeit with a couple of bright spots – in the US, the number of 'unicorn' start-ups reached a new high, and there remained a healthy volume of high-value ($100m or more) investment rounds. A slowdown in the US was, at least, consistent, with VC deals falling for the third consecutive quarter.

From then on, it got worse, right?

It did not get worse. The Q3 MoneyTree™ Report revealed that Q3 investment in US-based VC-backed companies reached $36.5 billion, the second-strongest quarter ever reported.

The good news was not confined to the US: funding to start-ups in Asia rose 74% in a quarter; in Europe, start-up funding jumped 29%.

The deals are happening. Read about them. Picture the exchange, cash moving from one person to another. Why is the exchange happening? What got them to that point? And could you get to that point, too?

WHERE US BANKS ARE BETTING ON FINTECH

US bank-backed deals to fintech startups by category, 2010 – 2020 YTD (8/27/20)

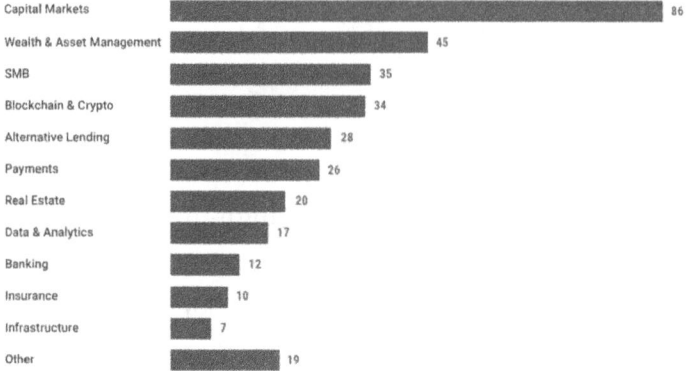

Category	Deals
Capital Markets	86
Wealth & Asset Management	45
SMB	35
Blockchain & Crypto	34
Alternative Lending	28
Payments	26
Real Estate	20
Data & Analytics	17
Banking	12
Insurance	10
Infrastructure	7
Other	19

CBINSIGHTS

Executive summary

Q1 2020

US Insights

US VC deal activity declines in Q1'20, but mega-rounds drive increase in funding

US VC deals fall for the third consecutive quarter in Q1'20: Deal activity for US VC-backed companies falls 9% QoQ and 16% YoY. In March 2020, US deals decrease 22% YoY, with some of the decline likely attributable to the earlier COVID-19 pandemic. Nonetheless, funding still rises 14% QoQ on the back of larger deals.

Nearly half of all US funding in Q1'20 comes from mega-rounds: Despite a slowdown in deals at the end of the quarter, 58 US companies raise rounds worth $100M or more in Q1'20, close to the record of 67 in Q2'19. 21 of these rounds took place in March 2020, suggesting COVID-19's impact may become more apparent in Q2'20.

The number of unicorn companies reaches a new high, but aggregate valuation is falling: The number of VC-backed startups valued at $1B+ continues to rise, hitting 204 private companies in Q1'20. However, aggregate valuation dips for the second consecutive quarter, to $624B.

Geographic Insights

Global deal activity and funding see YoY declines

North America, Asia, and Europe see combined funding of $50B in Q1'20: Global VC funding falls 10% in Q1'20 compared to Q1'19.

Asia sees the largest drop in funding, deal activity: Asia deal activity declines 20% YoY, compared to declines of 17% in North America and 10% in Europe, with some of the decline likely attributable to the earlier outbreak of COVID-19 pandemic. Funding to startups in Asia falls 19% YoY.

Atlanta, St. Louis, and Boston Metros hit eight-quarter highs for funding activity: Atlanta Metro funding increases to $540M in Q1'20, driven by two $200M+ mega-rounds, while St. Louis Metro funding reaches $412M. Boston Metro sees a 19% YoY increase in funding, rising to $3.5B.

The largest deals in the US all come from Silicon Valley: Despite a 12% YoY decrease in deal activity, the top five funding rounds in the US are all Silicon Valley startups that raised $450M+ each.

US VC funding in Q3'20 is second highest ever

US deals and dollars – Quarterly

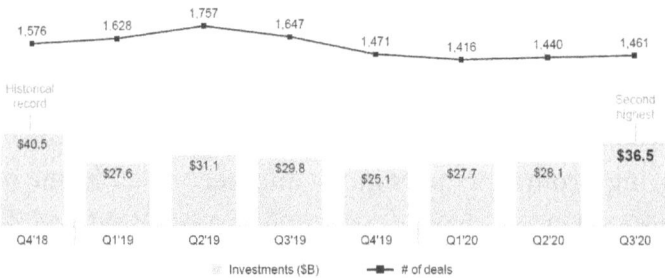

	Q4'18	Q1'19	Q2'19	Q3'19	Q4'19	Q1'20	Q2'20	Q3'20
# of deals	1,576	1,628	1,757	1,647	1,471	1,416	1,440	1,461
Investments ($B)	$40.5	$27.6	$31.1	$29.8	$25.1	$27.7	$28.1	$36.5

Historical record — $40.5

Second highest — $36.5

Investments ($B) — # of deals

Source: PwC/CB Insights MoneyTree™ Report Q3 2020

This is a clarifying exercise. It may throw open ideas and beckon you down paths you have not travelled before. But how do you know if these ideas and paths are right for your business?

Don't reach for it just yet

Don't pick up the phone or start devising an email campaign. We are not at that stage yet. For the moment, resist action: critical thinking must come first.

Critical thinking about opportunities will, ultimately, mean making choices about how you spend your time. Will one opportunity require much more from you to manage? If so, is it worth it?

Your business will have ambitions, abilities, and limitations.

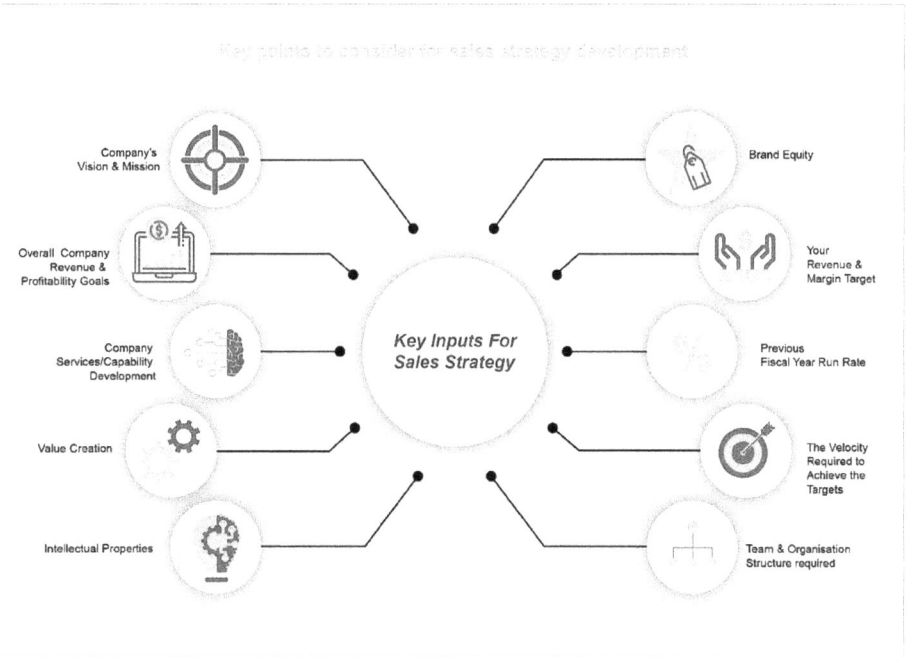

Key points to consider for sales strategy development

The preceding chart is a starting point for looking with clarity at these. It is also prism through which to view existing accounts. If you have a difficult client – one that seems to draw ceaselessly on your resources – then assess how they fit with brand, profitability, mission, and value creation. It may spark an interesting debate!

A word of caution on capability development. News of competitors moving in new directions may tempt you towards a 'me too' effort. They're investing, and it may look exciting, but a diffuse approach is very tricky to succeed with. Tread carefully.

A structured approach to the target client list

The target client list is a key output of sales strategizing, and central to the sales team's work: it should be treated as the most precious document! But it is only as good as the thought that has gone into it.

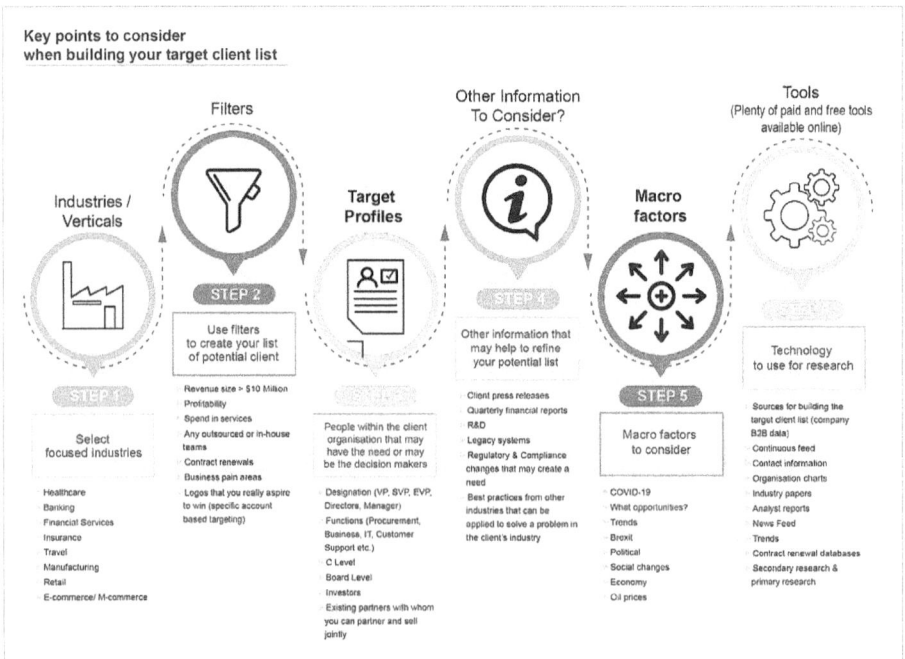

Key points to consider when building your target client list

Such is the wealth of information available, it is wise to harness technological tools, some of which have been designed for businesses like yours. Omdia, for example, focuses on technology markets research and consulting, and also offers vendor selection tools and research, which may be relevant for understanding the competitive landscape.

At the later stages, research includes compiling prospect contact details. Inaccurate information – email addresses or names that are out-of-date – not only wastes time, but it is also likely to reflect poorly on you, and at the first point of contact, too. Fortunately, there are a number of great resources available for building contact data of the highest integrity. Look at and compare the B2B sales and pipeline services offered by, to name a few, ZoomInfo, Lusha, RocketReach, and LinkedIn Sales Navigator. Think carefully about what would be most efficient for your business: you may only require access to a database, or you may find the leads and sales management tools available are a great starting point. The user experience will be a factor in your decision-making, because compiling prospect details requires very active search capabilities – both online, and with you.

The screen time is going to clock up

As a child, your parents may have issued dire warnings about the perils of looking at a computer or television screen for too many hours or trying to read books in semi-darkness. While I always advocate good lighting, it is important to let go any semblance of guilt about time spent in front of relevant reporting, both internal and external.

Effective strategy is built on understanding, and this understanding is enhanced with learning and research. Try thinking of your desk as a portal into a vast business-centred library, full of information. This will include trade magazines relevant to your target industries. But it may be that you have only been down one or two aisles and are missing some good stuff elsewhere. Think about the resources, free and paid, that you are using now. Are they enough? Is there a new subscription you would benefit from?

TOP TIP

Be aware of how your emotions change when considering existing accounts and different industries. If you are harbouring frustrations, or burning ambitions, (or both!), these will likely have a big influence on your decisions. Note what your feelings are and reflect on them.

Getting comfortable with numbers

Targets are not the only numbers you should be thinking about.

If a sales team or strategy is newly established, look closely at how you monitor the metrics. This is likely to start with the number of emails sent and calls made and conclude with the conversion rate. Look for ways of tracking activity more efficiently and ensure sales team contributors take responsibility for reporting it.

Internal reporting

Internal financial reporting is, by its nature, retrospective, with monthly and quarterly reporting, but it is highly relevant whether looking ahead (strategic planning) or looking back (business review).

The meaning of profit and loss is almost ingrained in our natures, and most people in business understand that the profit and loss account does not portray the movement of cash. But make sure you consider each prospect and each account in terms of profit, loss, and margin, too.

Your finance team guy or gal should be able to provide absolute clarity on the profitability of an existing account, and forward projections on a contract, too. If they are not already providing it, ask for this reporting, and if anything is unclear, ask again. A modern, high-calibre accountant should be fully prepared to explain what is happening behind the numbers – for example, why a profit turned to a loss, or an expense is so high – and be able to explain using clear, non-technical language. The best accountants are not just number crunchers, they are business partners.

External reporting

Another aspect of financial reporting, and one important in building a picture of a target client, is the balance sheet. Notes in the accounts, being regulated, can also be revealing – so do read them carefully!

Demand generation in a digital world

Part of your sales strategy is the 'shop front', which, being online, is not going to mean elegant signage and windows.

The challenge with every business operating online is that, unlike a bricks-and-mortar counterpart on a local high street, customers are not going to pass its door by accident. A B2B entity needs to say "I'm here," to the right people, in a way that is professional and efficient.

Appearing on the first page of a Bing or Google search is one way of saying "I'm here," and it is important your website build and creation includes attention to SEO (search engine optimisation). Behind Google's search engine is technology that assesses every website by measuring a variety of factors, including speed of loading, key words, and quality of content. This is an effort to ensure only the most valuable and relevant websites appear to their users.

You may want to hire an SEO expert, but if you are not already familiar with SEO basics, it is worth putting aside an hour or two to learn about them – there are good free resources on the topic, like this one from Moz.com – https://moz.com/beginners-guide-to-seo

Your website copy should compound that 'I'm here' message, with language that clearly communicates what you do. You will need to show a level of discretion, but clarity is king. Look at your competitors: you may want to do some things in a similar vein or distinguish yourself from them in other ways. Be aware of the subtle distinctions between US and UK spelling – choose one which makes sense for your audience and stick to it.

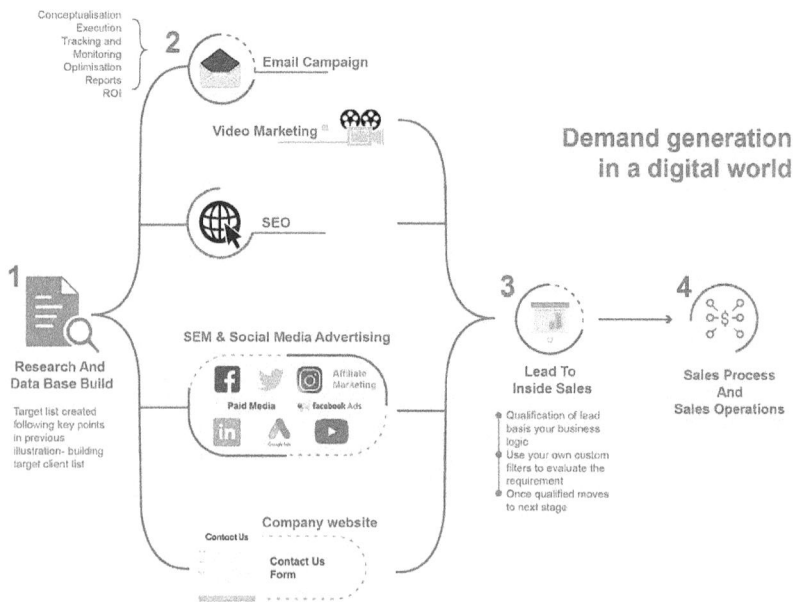

Paid media and email campaigns are part of your outreach work. A campaign may be where a target client sees your name for the first time, and you want that first impression to be the best impression, so think about specialist resources that may benefit you: a copywriter will

craft language that really speaks to your audience; designers work on imagery, layout and user experience. Don't stint on what you need.

Google remains the world's most popular search engine. An early marketing step is to register with Google My Business – it is free, and it means a respectable listing, including your location and a description of your services, will appear prominently when users search for your business name, or use words included in it. Once registered, you then have easy access to paid advertising through Google Ads. It is user-friendly– you can set a cap on spend, and access to daily analytics makes it easy to monitor click-throughs and conversion rates. It is easy to adjust your copy, call to action and locations where you want to advertise. Be prepared to trial a few different approaches and find what works for you.

2

WINNING PROCESSES
WIN CLIENTS

t is a marathon. From the first notification of a lead to the signing of a deal, from the first mile to twenty-sixth, performing requires rigour, discipline, and ambition.

I have mentioned ambition before. Ambition in sales may be interpreted in different ways. One kind of ambition is the desire for big contracts, prestigious clients, and a successful business. This type of ambition concerns the end results. It is a marathon time of two hours something, and the medal and prize that follows.

This should sit along another kind of ambition, one that is not just about the end result, but the path to it. There is more creativity and heart with this kind of ambition, which is why I think of a film director looking through the lens, and the people around him making sure the lighting is perfect, the set is perfect, the actor's clothing is perfect. Ambition is not just about goals; it is also about standards.

In a sales environment, standards and processes may be one and the same. We are aiming for a) uniformity and b) the highest quality, in every event in the sales process.

The value of research

You have a meeting in the diary – your first with your prospect. Great! Thorough research beforehand will help ensure that crucial first meeting runs smoothly.

The company

Be familiar with their products and services. Scour publicly available material about the company, including the annual accounts, and media coverage, and look out for the initiatives they are taking, their objectives and vision – these indicate where their focus and future investment will be.

Consider the numbers shown in their financial reporting. Is the profit and loss and balance sheet healthy? Could cost-cutting be on the horizon?

The person

Their profile will quickly establish their experience and background, but we need to look a little closer.

Conversation flows when people feel comfortable, when each person feels that the person opposite understands where they are coming from. So, it is valuable to identify common connections, which will be evident on a social network like LinkedIn, or even by looking at the company's history of acquisitions and investments.

During a first meeting, the sales leader may ask "Do you know…?" naming a common connection. The prospect's face brightens. "Yes! I work with him. He is the vice-president of marketing…"

You can picture it – rapport established, and quickly. When meeting someone new, a common connection is valuable. Don't waste the opportunity.

If you are not aware of any common connections, look for other commonalities that will help break the ice. This can be as simple as a common location. Perhaps they have blogged about living in Canada, and it so happens that you holidayed in Canada last year. You know how beautiful it is in the summer months – so talk about it!

Don't delegate the research

Pre-sales support may not be incentivised in the same way you are. They also may not have the same understanding you do, so don't leave the details to chance. Be involved – checking and reviewing thoroughly. It is your deal. Don't let it be controlled by someone else.

If the first meeting is successful, your sales team associates will be engaging with the prospect over the coming months. High quality engagement will help ensure the right solutions are pitched, and in the right way.

Salesperson or domain expert?

If your brand were only visible through a lens, what would a prospect see? If they see a salesperson touting a sales pitch, then the price (specifically, getting the lowest price) becomes their primary interest. This is because they don't see the value. This is a dangerous spot for a supplier: the prospect is likely to leave the equitable ground of deal-making and think only bargain-hunting.

As an alternative, domain led sales command premium pricing, and increase the strength of engagement throughout the sales process.

Domain led sales start with domain expertise, but this must be apparent. Make sure your sales contributors understand the data flows of the prospect or client's customers. They should also be aware of – and sensitive to – the client's budgetary outlook. Being informed on both these points will ensure the client is offered relevant solutions.

Get to know the client's ecosystem

It is not too early to start compiling a picture of the internal workings of a prospective client entity; indeed, an understanding of the client's ecosystem will help immeasurably in smoothing the progress of a Request for Proposal (RFP).

The organisational chart is the barest beginnings. Relationship mapping (covered in detail in Chapter 4) recognises the various important and influential players within an organisation, beyond the vice-presidents and directors shown on their website.

TOP TIP

Hold some meetings off-site. This is where contacts are going to be able to talk more openly about their challenges, stakeholders, and other topics relevant to a proposal. Off-site meetings are also discreet – keeping you one step ahead of the competition.

Understand the buying process

You know that the RFP must be approved by decision-makers in different jurisdictions: the sales director, the head of product, and the head of engineering. Look at the following example:

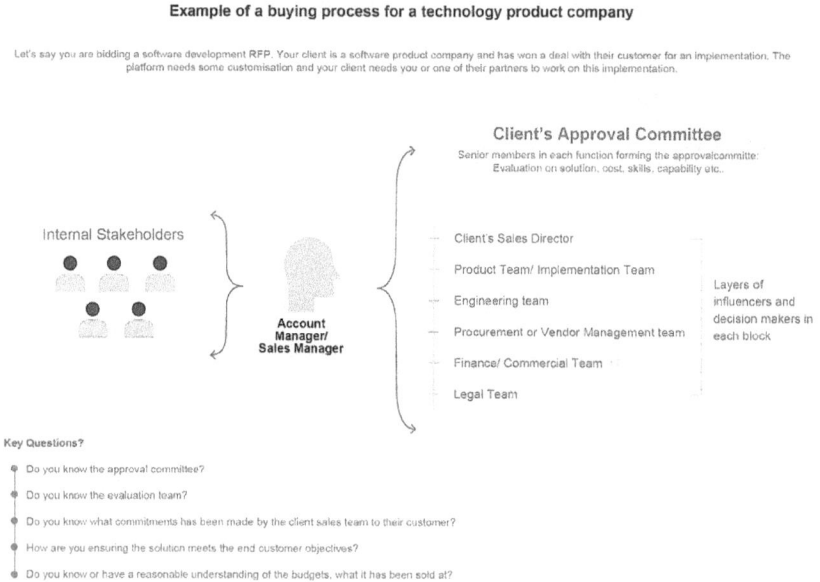

Example of a buying process for a technology product company

Let's say you are bidding a software development RFP. Your client is a software product company and has won a deal with their customer for an implementation. The platform needs some customisation and your client needs you or one of their partners to work on this implementation.

Client's Approval Committee
Senior members in each function forming the approvalcommitte:
Evaluation on solution, cost, skills, capability etc..

Internal Stakeholders

Account Manager/ Sales Manager

Client's Sales Director
Product Team/ Implementation Team
Engineering team
Procurement or Vendor Management team
Finance/ Commercial Team
Legal Team

Layers of influencers and decision makers in each block

Key Questions?
- Do you know the approval committee?
- Do you know the evaluation team?
- Do you know what commitments has been made by the client sales team to their customer?
- How are you ensuring the solution meets the end customer objectives?
- Do you know or have a reasonable understanding of the budgets, what it has been sold at?

After an RFP has been met with approval by different operational leaders, negotiations with Procurement and Legal start. These different voices form an approval committee of sorts. But do you know the people who have sight of the RFP? And the order in which they will see it?

This detailed knowledge will help you craft an RFP that meets the requirements of each decision-maker. But don't let this awareness oppress or limit you. Be confident. Have your style; they should know it's you.

How good is the proposal – really?

Adhering closely to a defined, documented process (like that shown in the following chart) is a strong indicator of good governance, helping to keep your sales team safe from confusion or mishaps.

Sales process & sales operations

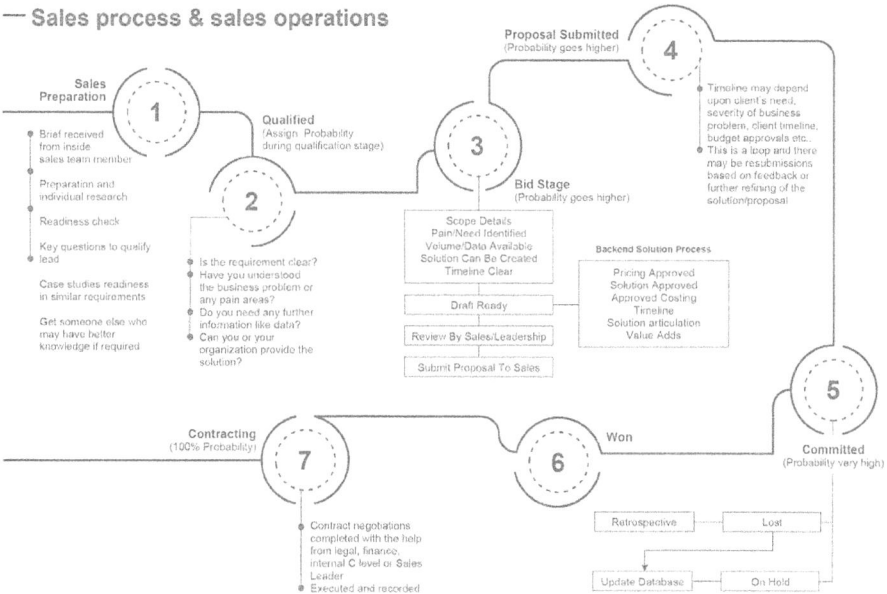

But we are humans, too, subject to all the variability of human emotion. Sometimes we need to look beyond the documents and emails.

CASE STUDY:
A growing European company

Graham returned from China in triumph. 'The deal is done!' he declared. I had sent Graham to China, and the Philippines, for site visits with the vendor manager of a new, fast-growing European company as part of the proposal process. Graham's trip went well, but the vendor manager must have made some promises beyond his remit, which was limited to evaluating our sites, their location, existence, and then quality.

Graham was a smart guy, but he overlooked the buying process. The deal went on hold for almost three months with no specific feedback.

I decided to meet Tony, the executive sponsor of the company, in person. He was due to be in Berlin on business. I asked Graham to set up a dinner meeting at a venue of my choice, and both the reservation and meeting were secured.

When we met Tony, he was accompanied by his team. The menu arrived, and I gave Tony the wine list.

"Tony, please go ahead. Feel free," I said.

"Okay, JT, what should I choose?" he said.

"That depends on what you are going to decide tonight," I said, jokingly. He looked at me and smiled. "Just go with what your heart tells you," I insisted.

The food arrived, and we started talking. Pleasantries at first, but before another glass of wine flowed, I posed a very direct question.

"Tony, what is stopping you working with us?" I asked. He said he did not have absolute confidence in the English language skills of our staff based in the offshore location. His current supplier was working out of South Africa, he felt the teams there spoke better English.

"Tony, here is the deal. I have such confidence in the English language skills of our staff in the offshore location, that I will offer a three-month pilot. Let us define the service level agreements, and if at the end of the first three months we have not met them, you don't have to pay a penny."

Tony was taken aback. Graham stared at me, shocked. I had showed my conviction, however, and it made an impression.

"Okay, I'll think over it," Tony said. "Absolutely, not a penny?"

"Not a penny."

Later that evening, before we went separate ways, I offered to show him the offshore site.

"That should be our next step," I said.

Two weeks later, he called me. He was going to travel to see things for himself. It would be his first visit to this offshore city.

"I'm coming with you," I said.

He saw the site – we let him interact with our people, let him experience the company culture, take in local cultures, and we let him evaluate the English language skills, too. Away from the office, we had a good time, squeezed in some time for sightseeing! At the end of the trip, we hugged.

"Okay, the deal is done," he said.

We signed a multi-million, multi-year customer service deal. This company was an innovative and fast-growing company – they were not risk averse – yet they still needed strong assurance to progress. I did not, however, try to second-guess their reasons for holding back. You will notice that I asked a very direct question, "What is stopping you working with us?" And I was very deliberate about how I asked it: we were not facing each other in an austere meeting room, for example, and there had been enough engagement beforehand to warrant the question.

Make the "next steps" clear to the prospect. What if I had not offered to show Tony our site? It would have been very easy for the deal to effectively go on hold again, with no positive move forward on either side, and Tony's days filling up with other, more attractive things to do. An invitation to visit the site underlined my confidence in the product and service being offered, a confidence already demonstrated by my offer to run a three-month pilot. Ask yourself, are you proud of your products and services Do you believe in them? And are you demonstrating that belief?

3

THE SELF-AWARE LEADER

The waiter said the words slowly, quietly.

"Your card has been declined."

I was attempting to pay a four-figure bill at the Ducasse in Park Lane. I was surrounded by clients. And it was 1 o' clock in the morning. The most senior (in terms of designation and authority), and owner of a millions of dollars software development budget, saw my predicament.

"Do you want me to take care of this? We can sort it out lately," he said, lips barely moving, like a ventriloquist.

"No, no, just give me a moment." I called my accountant. Thankfully, he picked up.

"What are you doing?" I said.

"I'm sleeping."

"The card you gave me has just been declined. You get in your car and come over here to sort this out."

He lived in Greater London towards Heathrow and it was at least an hour plus drive with no traffic.

"Oh..." A realisation – the corporate credit card he had given me had expired. The card he should have given me was at home with him, in a trouser pocket.

I gave the phone to the waiter, who was able to put through an offline transaction. Still, the story followed me everywhere. It became a legend. "I hope your card is working," people joked and I always smiled, taking it all in The story became so famous that clients who had not been part of that dinner meeting also took at dig at me.

Challenges and surprises confront us at the most inopportune moments. Even relatively minor mistakes – like my accountant giving me an expired corporate card and me not checking it before – can have embarrassing consequences.

My card being declined at the Ducasse amused my colleagues, but had I handled it differently – become flustered at the table, or yelled down the phone at an accountant still in his pyjamas – it would probably not have been a funny story, or one colleagues would have wanted to mention again.

Both self-awareness and confidence are essential for a leader, entrepreneur, and salesperson. As business grows, you will grow with it. Much will be asked of you. You will also be exposed to new personalities, demands, even crises. You need to be ready for them.

Under the influence

I'm not talking about alcohol; I don't consume alcohol. I'm talking about the influence customers, colleagues, and bosses will have on you. Customers will show you what they value.

I was in a business review with client senior executives, who were expressing their deep unhappiness at service levels were not being met. In an effort to remedy the situation and retain the customer, an action plan had been presented. I had seen it, and it consisted of small changes here and there – retrain this guy, reshuffle that team. I thought it to be a series of superficial fixes, a plan that did not address the root problems. I had raised my concerns and suggested alternative solutions as it was being drafted, but, frustratingly, they had not been included in the plan.

During the review, I saw the client's body language and understood that they were not convinced by the plan. I saw clearly that they did not believe we could turn around the situation.

"We need to do a complete reboot," I said. A bold and unequivocal statement, and not one anyone expects to hear from a service provider. The most senior executive leaned back in his chair. He is softly spoken at any time, and I had surprised him. After a spell of quiet, he turned to me again.

"JT, I appreciate your honesty." He was listening. We were 30 days into a 90-day termination notice. I needed more than 60 days to implement the wholesale changes necessary. I needed to negotiate an extension, which I did. We retained the contract.

Episodes like that inform you. And they are a reminder that, ultimately, we don't compete with the strength of offers or functionality; we compete with the strength of our people.

You learn from customers, and colleagues too, about what to do, and, potentially, what not to do. In my early career as a sales professional, our team leader taught me what not to do. I saw him boasting to his boss, taking credit for a new deal that I and other colleagues had worked hard on. He had never attended a single meeting. He didn't go to meetings when I invited him!

It was petty, frustrating behaviour, brought about by insecurity. Hampered by a lack of understanding of the environment he was in; he did not sell anything. (And make no mistake, sales team leaders should be selling, too.)

Not knowing things is nothing to be ashamed of. Not knowing things, yet making no effort to learn, even though it is impacting on your performance... that is different.

Managing without a particular technical expertise

A senior job role may mean talking to technical experts wielding in-depth knowledge, and in a field that is not your own. If you have managerial and budget responsibilities, listening to, or being part of a conversation that is basically meaningless to your ears is going to feel uncomfortable!

It may be that you can manage and perform perfectly well without becoming familiar with those unfamiliar words and concepts. But being periodically baffled is going to limit your engagement with the people involved, which at a minimum is going to make your work less fun.

Thrown into a new setting, I have immersed myself in technical books, so I could get up to speed. Another very effective way of getting a handle on a topic is by spending time with the experts. Plan a couple of hours sitting with them at work – much can be picked up from their day-to-day – or ask someone. You can say, "Explain it to me." Many people will be happy to show off their knowledge!

I met a client as part of work on a new RFP (Request for Proposal). He managed software which calculated aircraft weight and balance. He was talking to me about this specific aircraft technology, which I was new to, when he looked at me.

"You are managing software development projects, and... you don't know anything?"

"I'm not technical," I said. "But, yes, I am managing this relationship. If you've got five minutes, then why don't we sit together, and you can explain it to me."

Five minutes became 45 minutes, but this was the start of a good working relationship. It is just about your approach – being humble and making the effort to learn. Eventually, you will be able to speak the customer's language.

What do you need?

You should know where you excel, and where you need additional support. What is too difficult, time-consuming or risky to take on yourself? The list is likely to grow as your responsibilities do. And do you know where to find those resources?

Trusted hands make the most significant challenges manageable. Having the right resources is part of good governance, too. Having technical expertise on hand will help you craft solutions with confidence.

Don't wait for something to go wrong to seek legal support. If something is a worry, seek advice – that is what the experts are there for! Maintain those relationships, too: you don't want to be the guy who only appears when there is a problem.

Having the right support is not, however, an excuse for ignorance. "Limitation of liability" is subject to negotiation in the contract for a new deal. When I started, the phrase was a mystery, but I sat down with a lawyer and made the effort to understand it. Then I could take a query about it with confidence, which strengthened my rapport with the client, and put me in a better place for negotiating.

Going to the right source at the right time is a skill. If you are finding the talent and professionalism you need, well done. And if you haven't yet, it is time to go out looking for it.

4

ACCOUNT MANAGEMENT
FOR GROWTH

S trong account management is key to healthy client relationships, increasing sales and growing wallet share.

It is also demanding. You may begin as one of 50 suppliers, one who just takes orders. You want a spot as a preferred supplier. Successful account management changes the client's perceptions of you. This change in perceptions is a climb up the value chain, as shown in the following chart. It requires deliberate, sustained focus on the quality of relationships.

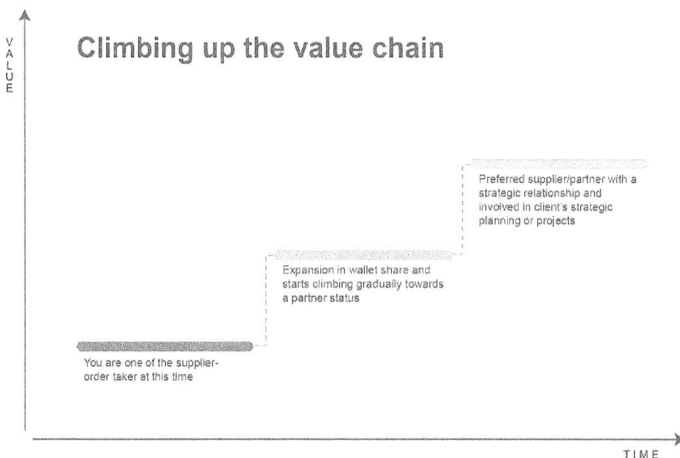

Climbing up the value chain

VALUE

Preferred supplier/partner with a strategic relationship and involved in client's strategic planning or projects

Expansion in wallet share and starts climbing gradually towards a partner status

You are one of the supplier-order taker at this time

TIME

I'm fine where I am, thanks

What happens if you stay in the bottom corner? Perhaps your predecessor was content in this lowly place – or just did not know how to get out of it – and you have their 'inheritance', in which case you know just how grim it is. If you're not sure what this dark place looks like, the signs of bad account management are:

- High receivables – your invoices are paid late or not at all.
- Relationships are singular – the client is a medium-sized or large organisation, but when you ask for contacts, you only get one or two names.
- No clarity of client's business objectives and strategic plans – no one knows what is on the horizon for the client. The account manager is unable to provide key updates or insights
- No proper governance.
- Very quick escalations from client.
- Unsigned statement of works (SOW) or contracts.
- Inability to get meetings.
- No connect between senior leadership of supplier with senior leaders of client.
- Lack of understanding of the client's buying process cycle.
- Weak internal collaboration/ minimal or no teamwork.

Here, you are a commodity, judged only on price: a very precarious place to be. Without a concerted effort, a situation like this is an inevitability.

To get out of it, we need to build relationships. But that instruction 'build relationships' is heard so often in so many places. Its meaning, and how we action it, is easily lost. What do we really mean by it, in the context of account management?

We want to move from singular relationships (a sign of account management sickness, shown above) to broad and fruitful connections with the client. Our efforts must be focused. Who are the decision-makers and influencers at the client? And how well do you know them? These questions are at the heart of relationship mapping.

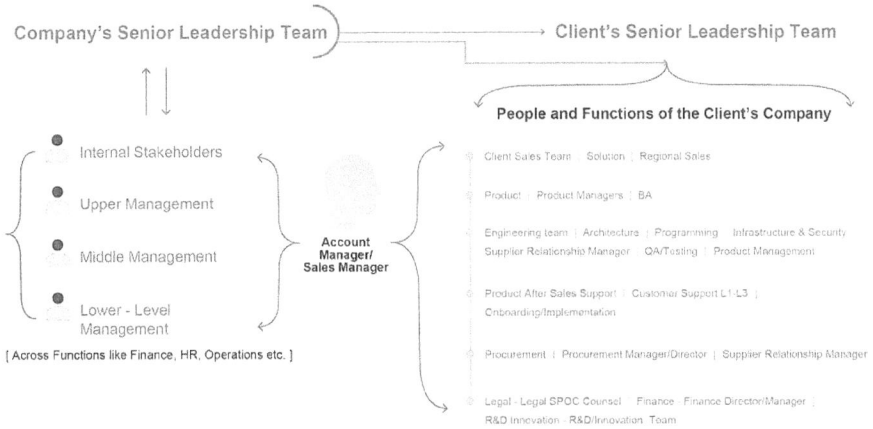

An example of a relationship mapping

You may want to begin with a relationship heat map. This is your client's organisational chart, with each key position and personality shown. Consider, in each case, whether they are:

a) Supportive of your business (Green)
b) Neutral about your business (Amber)
c) Not in favour of your business (Red), or
d) You have not established a connection with them (Grey)

After this exercise, it may be that the relationship heat map looks a little dismal. Fortunately, there is a lot the account manager can do.

Leverage existing contacts

An existing relationship introducing you creates an infinitely more precious new connections than a cold email that reads "Hi, I'm…"

Start with your existing contacts, even if it is only a handful of people. Ask "Who should I speak to?" with a view to managing projects or identifying scope for more. What you are aiming for is "Go meet X, go meet Y." If you are honest, if you are transparent, the people you work with will be willing to help.

TOP TIP

Corridor conversations with clients are important, as are coffee breaks. Allow space for them. Away from the desk, and away from the office, open conversation is likely to yield better results.

Account manager as an enabler

Nobody wants to behave clumsily or insensitively in a corporate environment – the proverbial bull in a china shop – so you won't find people reaching out to, and within, a client's organisation of their own accord.

The account manager must be an enabler, connecting the right people, or making sure they know they have the freedom to connect. Make meetings meaningful, with a strategic meeting of minds.

TOP TIP

Take your expert to a relevant meeting. An enthusiastic, highly knowledgeable contact will demonstrate your brand's domain expertise, impressing the client, and enhancing perceptions of your business. How are you enabling relationships between client stakeholders and your internal stakeholders?

Relationship mapping in numbers

My Christmas card list surprised the marketing team. It had more than 50 names on it. All were personnel at a single client's organisation, and I was only one year into managing the relationship.

That Christmas, the Finance team were also vocal, grumbling about the high number greetings cards that were going out. But there was a clear correlation between growing connections at the client and increasing sales. Why? Because healthy relationships help you identify sales opportunities and applicable solutions, and they enhance your positioning – your place in the client's mind.

Face to face with the senior leadership team

Strive for meetings between client leadership and your own – it strengthens commitment. But know when to call it. Do you merit their attention yet? This is when wallet share is highly relevant.

CASE STUDY:
A UK and Europe-based hospitality brand

When we met this prospect, they were looking to increase the scale of their existing outsourcing strategy, and unhappy with their current vendors. A lot of their dissatisfaction seemed to stem from the quality of communication. They felt issues being raised were going unheard, and problem-solving measures inadequate. Another notable source of discontent was a lack of attention and focus from the existing vendor's leadership team. So, if you think clients don't notice such things, they do!

We recommended a right-shoring approach, and a detailed evaluation of skills and locations followed. Four sites and locations were selected for study, and due diligence conducted. Importantly, the hospitality brand's vendor manager was allowed an open and transparent site visit, with no scripting of any sort. Both parties invested time and money in this evaluation process. It was thorough.

The evaluation process was also very structured. Respective stakeholders were assigned for each part of the process for each site, making communication straightforward and efficient.

From the onset of the evaluation process, the prospective client was allowed access to the top leadership team. This shows a level of dedication and respect, which will make an impression with a prospect. At this stage, our CEO had a face-to-face meeting with the prospect, taking an intercontinental flight to meet them. This demonstrated his personal commitment. The meeting was also an opportunity for the CEO to outline his focus areas and vision, allowing the prospect to become much better acquainted with a new vendor and their values.

The account growth plan

The account growth plan is a living document, in which your strategy is laid bare: producing it is an intensive exercise. Some of the themes we have already touched on will be shown in it – the client's buying pattern, relationship maps and client data flows. Some other topics which should feature in a basic plan are:

- Client's long-term and short-term vision
- Client's business objectives
- Client budgets – where are they allocating their funds?
- Your strategy based on your company's vision, goals and targets
- Solutions – what solutions are you creating to solve client's problems? Are you self-sufficient? Do you need to create any other solutions? Do you need partners to create the solutions?
- Governance plan – internal and external

Self-monitoring for success

Self-monitoring is part of taking responsibility, and a strong account manager monitors their progress against their target. Looking beyond the target, how are you doing? Find out with the Account Manager's Health Check.

ACCOUNT MANAGER'S HEALTH CHECK

- Do you understand your client's product or services well?
- Do you understand the client's data flows? For example, the process before and after a sale of your client's product.
- What is your hook for account longevity/ stickiness? Why should your client work with you?
- Do you have an account growth plan?
- Where is the client assigning budgets for the year or following year/s?
- Are you aware of organisational changes at client side? Are you anticipating them?
- What happens if your main sponsor is sacked or moves on?
- Is there anyone to guide you or facilitate any meetings with new stakeholders in the client organisation?
- Does the client provide you with regular information about what is happening within their organisation?
- Are you tracking your KPIs and numbers on a daily basis? Do you have the numbers at your fingertips?
- Are you looking outside of the client's industry to look for best practices?
- Do you go to your client with suggestions? These may not have a monetary value to them, but they do help build positive perceptions. They emphasise that you are very much connected to the client's success and their goals.
- Is your internal sales process easy for the client?

5

CHANGING MINDS

James managed all partners and suppliers from his European city office. For the first six months of my tenure as the account manager, he was as remote as the moons of Mars. Queries that should have gone to me, he addressed to my boss. He was dismissive of invites; I could not get a meeting with him.

One day, he called me. I had not informed him of a new project development, he said. I let him talk. The minutes ticked by, while he detailed the extent and significance of this grievance.

"I have made so many attempts to try to talk to you," I said. "I have tried to reach out, to establish a connection. You have never given me a platform. Did I not request it?"

"Yes," he admitted.

"It is my job to grow this business," I went on. "We work out of different cities, but if you give me the platform, I will take it. I'm not stupid. I know I cannot bypass you."

I made it clear that I understood his authority, and was not trying to undermine him.

"You give me the forum," I said, "And we will put a proper process in place." A moment's silence, while he took this in.

"Okay. Fair enough. Fridays are good for me. How much time do you need?"

"Half an hour would be enough."

We met every Friday for the next five years except when we were out of office. When I was leaving the business, he told me he would miss me.

The story is a reminder that your name's meaning and value is not fixed. It can change, and it will, according to the experience clients have with you and your team. And when I say name, I don't mean the company name, the one that is on a wall outside. I mean your own name, the name printed inside your passport, because your name, and your face, represents the company.

CASE STUDY:
A cruise liner based in the US

I had come into responsibility for the North America region for only a week when I got an urgent call from a US-based colleague.

"The vice-president of product has called me," he said. "He says he is going to sue us." Our software engineering, design and analytics team were building an algorithm based airfare booking system that would help reduce the cost of air travel. I was told that delivery of the software was five months late.

I had a call with the head of engineering, whose team was delivering the project, my US-based colleague, and our chief operating officer (COO). I was told that the customer's requirements were regularly changing, which extended the timeline. I arranged to fly out to the US, but beforehand asked that a call be arranged with just me and the customer.

"I have just taken over this region," I said. "I'm sorry that our first call is in these circumstances. I just want to hear from you what exactly the problem is."

He gave me a laundry list of problems. Before leaving for the US, I spoke with internal teams. In the US, I met with the client's CIO and his peers at their office and then we headed for lunch. They were so full of complaints that I could not eat my lunch! But these were problems that could be solved.

As had been indicated internally, scope creep was evident. But there was more to it. Our teams would action changes but not flag them through a change management process, or show the work done to the client.

We deployed more audit trails and traceability, so that changes to scope were clear, and ensured we could track them. We also needed to ensure the customer had more visibility of the team's progress: "We have developed this in the last two weeks, let us show you' is a good exchange to have."

The engineering and design teams were straying into commercial discussions whenever they saw the requirement changing.

"That will cost you extra," they would say – very annoying for a customer.

I made it very clear that it is the account managers that talk about money; the design and engineering teams do not engage in commercial discussions. The language used in commercial and delivery teams must be distinct.

All the problem-solving measures were in place within weeks. We were able to recover the extra costs involved in serving the customer, which they were happy to pay. Furthermore, the annual value of the account eventually doubled.

It would be easy to greet customer complaints with weariness, and even suspicion. When I first became aware of this customer's complaint, they were already exasperated, their frustrations made clear by a threat to sue. Customers do, however, sign a contract, and while this brings about legal and even moral obligations, it also indicates their initial desire to work with you. In more strained moments, it is worth remembering what their intentions were at the outset, and what your intentions were. If these were favourable, complaints are actually an opportunity, not just to rectify emerging problems, but also to strengthen your working relationship.

Customer complaint-handling requires a diligent and investigatory approach: I needed to hear from all the relevant parties, both internally and at the client, in order to resolve the issues. But you will notice this process of discovery did not take very long – relatively short meetings were enough.

Don't be afraid of problems! The biggest problems are often also simple problems, as I found with the US cruise line. Whenever the design team warned, "That will cost extra," they had good intentions. However, because it was not accompanied by the appropriate discipline, they were only aggravating the client. Money is always a sensitive subject, and its discussion should be very controlled.

With James in Europe, and the US cruise line, building trust and overcoming resistance depended on polite but direct language, and action to support it. Meeting expectations and getting results is crucial, especially when something has gone awry. But what about when everything is going to plan? Most of the time, it should. There are still many opportunities to build trust and rapport.

Tell me more

Many of us have a special enthusiasm or interest beyond the workplace: a sport, a creative medium or a hobby to lose countless joyful, content hours in. If your colleague has a passion, they will probably name it, but it just as an aside – it was how they spent their Saturday morning, or its the reason for a forthcoming shopping trip. No one wants to burden or bore another with unasked-for details, so this bright light in their life is casually mentioned. It is just an aside.

If you say, "Tell me more," or words like it, they'll look at your face briefly, checking that you mean it and are not feigning interest to pass the time. You do mean it, so they start to talk, freely, and with real energy.

The conversation may prove illuminating. One of my clients had a great understanding and passion for cultivating wine. In a restaurant, he would be able to tell me about the history and geography of a particular wine and talk discerningly about the taste.

Taking an interest in other people's interests is a straightforward way to maintain friendly conversation. And since it is rarer than you might think, it helps 'stick' your name and face in your contact's mind. Also, try to let go any of self-consciousness about approaching a topic: I don't drink alcohol, but my client and I could still converse happily about vineyards.

6

CREATING AN OPTIMAL SALES ENVIRONMENT

Leadership has a special kind of visibility. If you are rising through the ranks, you are monitored by vigilant bosses. If you are a leader, you may still be monitored by an ever-vigilant boss or two, but your peers and those reporting to you are observing you too. What they see has an impact: the values a leader displays are extremely influential. The ideal values will lead to staff growing and excelling; the opposite will have them looking for a role elsewhere.

A developing team

Younger team players will look around them and assess themselves in comparison to their peers, and to you. If the standards are high, they'll be working to keep up. But you need to show them what 'good' looks like.

This applies to targets, of course, but there is scope for progress and achievement in other ways. Early in my career, I found myself making changes to the kind of dialogue I had with prospects, consciously shifting from 'salesperson' to a more consultative role. The latter has no stigma attached, easing conversations, but it requires a change in their perceptions of me.

It may be that team members are completely happy with their current outlook. But always be conscious of where they are in their career, and how they might benefit from having the freedom to do things differently. Show that you trust and respect them, and they will surprise you with their initiative, candour and progress.

Managing remuneration

It takes a certain type of person to be able to live with the pressure of making targets every day. Not everyone can do it. Travel and hours impact on personal and family life, too. When the pressures of work are felt more keenly, team members will be still more conscious of how they are being rewarded for their efforts. Remuneration can become a hot topic.

Make it your business to stay up to date with market rates, and maintain an awareness of the importance staff members will place on the fixed salary as a measure of how much the company values them. The commission part of their remuneration is an incentive to perform, so they will consider it differently. Your most loyal and valuable team contributors will allow time for remuneration to be reviewed, and they may display a degree of flexibility. But don't leave it too long.

Striving for efficient working practices and methods

As a sales leader, you have control not just over your own work, but that of others, too. Being able to spot and implement shifts and changes that makes things a little bit faster, tidier, or more productive is part of your value. It is important not to do this occasionally, or casually. A comprehensive and consistent drive for the healthiest and most efficient working is what I call pruning.

Imagine a gardener on a lavish country estate, diligently, carefully cutting and shaping the flowers and plants so that they are as strong, bright, and beautiful as any visitor would wish for. The gardener is pruning, the same way a sales leader or leadership team should be with their business.

It may be that a project, process or individuals are not yielding results. Yet they still consume resources. Leaders must view this wastefulness with the same clinical and, perhaps, ruthless eyes as the gardener does deadwood. And like the gardener, they must be active in treating or removing it. Pruning is deeply practical. Done continuously, this shapes the team or organisation, and helps make a progressive and profitable workplace.

I have talked about how pruning works for external matters, but it is applicable to one's own thought processes, too. Look at your attitude and behaviour. What is working? What gets results? And what is holding you back? Lose the habits that are non-productive.

TOP TIP

Have a look at your to-do list today. Are there any tasks on it which do not yield results? What would happen if you put a line through them?

Governance and control: observing legal and regulatory requirements

A management role often means new responsibility for safeguarding the assets of the company you work in. Oversights, like unsigned contracts or patchy processes around money and finance, do not make a manager a maverick, someone who is too cool to worry about signatures or approvals. Deliberately overlooking controls just means that manager is a risk.

Good governance and controls, including provisions around data protection, protect the company legally and financially. Being exposed is about more than the what the outside world might bring you – gaps in processes increase the risk of internal fraud. Pay attention to those auditors' recommendations, and how you might be able to look after your assets more: it could save a lot of pain in the long run.

7

CUSTOMER SAYS NO – OR DO THEY?

The sales team were at their very best. The meetings always went well. The proposal, honed to perfection, was beautiful. But the prospect has said, "No." What next?

In the introduction, I had the pleasure of debunking sales myths. One of those myths was that a salesperson needs a thick skin: they must simply be impervious to all the rejection and keep persisting. The implication is that they must be unrelenting, unassailable, and unmovable. One type of salesperson may behave like this. But the smarter salesperson hears "No" and seeks to understand it fully.

How well are you reading the client's emotions? Technology changes, but human behaviour has not. Buying is emotional. What emotions, positive and negative, might be in play?

Look behind the words. What is not being said? Clients have insecurities, prejudices, and frustrations, just like anyone else.

Keep their interests before your own, and these interrogating questions may yield interesting answers. Even if you cannot recover the sale, you will be able to get to the next one quicker by understanding WHY it is was a "No" this time, and learning to handle it. Reflect on the experience, and let it inform you.

The silly reasons

Bias has a role in decision-making, and its power can be evident from the very beginning. If a prospect is honest, you may discover that your proposal was declined for a silly reason: they have an opinion or perception that is unfair, baseless or outdated. When confronted with silly reasons, it is important to remember that, however silly the reason, you (usually) cannot change someone's mind about it. This bias is part of their brain's workings, and they're not going to reset the neural pathways and start thinking differently just for you. Sorry.

There are ways to avoid encountering this standstill situation too often. Are you mindful of what their position is likely to be? And how flexible can you be? Consider what you can and can't change in a proposal.

Fortunately, a deal is just as likely to get stuck in the works for a sound reason, and one that can be addressed. It might take some work trying to discover what that reason is, though. This was what happened with one client, based in the UK.

CASE STUDY:
A hospitality technology company

We were in talks to provide back office support – content creation and management. The deal had been with a colleague for some time without closing. We arranged that I would be introduced to the client, who represented the group, for lunch at an Indian restaurant.

With some gentle nudging in the right direction, the client revealed why he had stalled on a new deal. He said he was conscious of the risks of moving to a new supplier. They had been with their current supplier for over a decade, and our understanding was that they had done a good job. Yet our initial proposal had not included any risk mitigation. Drawing from my experience in managing operations and migrating projects, I started talking to him about all the risks at his side, and started mitigating them one by one at the lunch table. He listened closely and seemed to absorb my plan. Later, I followed through with a documentation of the same, along with a very detailed transition plan.

I did not have to do any selling – I was just addressing his concerns. With this client, I made use of my background and knowledge gained outside sales, and this enabled me to deal confidently with the particular details in this proposal. Within two months, we signed a multi-year and multi-million-dollar contract.

When operating in a sales capacity, don't lose sight of the experience you have gained in other, earlier roles, and as a manager in relevant fields – it may prove very helpful in guiding a prospect towards a deal.

8

IT IS TROUSERS, NOT PANTS

was at the airport with a colleague. We were waiting for another senior colleague.

"I shall be a fortune teller," I said. "I shall predict the future."

What did I see in the future? I described what our colleague would be wearing (colour, size, cut etc.) when he appeared.

Soon enough, a sartorial disaster matching my description, appeared. The suit jacket was slipping off one shoulder and the hems of his trousers were trailing. It was oversized and the colour of the suit always looked dull.

My guy looked at me. "How did you know?"

A senior salesperson, leader or C-suite professional may need to travel a lot; I have spent as many as three weeks out of every four visiting clients across the world. This makes attention to appearance even more important.

Crossing cultures and varying climates can make the right choices a bit more tricky. But that guy, with the too-big jacket and the too-long trousers – he didn't even know what size he was! Let us consider the clothes we wear, and with absolute seriousness – not as fashion journalists, but as professionals who want to make a good impression.

The right choices

You are in a department store – the SALE sign drew you through its doors – and see that on the rails are shirts, and they look good. Nice colours! Nice price! But are they right for you? There are a few things to consider.

Fit

Poorly fitting clothes, as well as looking bad, highlight even the slightest imperfections – if you are little bit short, or a little bit rounded, clothes that don't fit well signal these things very clearly. Know your measurements, or get measured professionally, and always try clothes on and assess fit. Don't rely on the labels, because shops and brands don't size consistently.

Fabric and materials

Clothes are made for the country and climate the shop is selling in. If you buy in the UK, the manufacturers and buyers are fully prepared for all the drizzle and damp a small island in the northern hemisphere contends with. If you take clothes and shoes from another part of the world to London's rain-soaked pavements, you may find they are not up to the task.

Several years ago, before I knew better, I bought a pair of boat shoes in Delhi. The brand's advertising included photos of mountains – these were 'mountain' boat shoes, according to the advert! I didn't take them up a mountain, but I did take them to London. They fell apart after two months.

Suitability for the occasion

Be wary of shiny, too bright or unusual-looking fabrics in the daytime – there is a clear distinction between day and evening attire. One time, I saw a guy wear a formal dinner jacket in an afternoon business meeting. It was like a tuxedo! He left a lasting impression, but it was for the wrong reasons.

When travelling and spending time with clients socially, look ahead and consider the itinerary carefully – there may be sports and social events you are unfamiliar with, and want to be appropriately attired for. Research, to find out what is expected, and choose clothing that is natural and comfortable for that environment.

If you need a beautiful dress or hat for an occasion, and in a country you only spend part of the year in, consider renting clothing from an online retailer. Clothes rental is so popular now that there is no stigma attached, and there are designer brands are easily available on some platforms. It is a cost-effective way to look the part – just be sure you allow enough time to try the size, and swap for another if needed.

Trends, fashion, and personal taste

In the larger stores, a vast floor (or two or three) of clothing can feel slightly overwhelming. Faced with seemingly limitless choices, it may be tempting to end the whole enterprise as quickly as possible by grabbing the first thing you see and hurrying to the till.

In advance of any shopping expedition, you should have a good idea of what you are looking for. This will make buying clothes a lot less stressful (and it may even be enjoyable!). Thankfully, there are lots of resources to help you. These are easily available, and from the comfort of home.

If you are new to European cities, do have a look at leading lifestyle magazines printed in the UK. Whatever machinations Brexit produces, the UK still has much in common with its neighbours. Men may want to look at GQ or Esquire, and magazines aimed at women include Vogue, Stylist, Red, and Prima.

Magazine photography and articles do sometimes focus on what the most prestigious fashion houses are doing, and those brands have an enormous influence on what will be produced for high street stores, so pay attention to the colours and patterns they are using, and the sort of values their choices espouse. Do they favour a sporty look? Or more traditional? Think about how you feel about the different styles.

The magazines also often print 'How to wear' pieces, and they indicate clearly what is popular. You can also browse current styles with websites dedicated to clothing and style, like Luxe Digital, Stitch Fix, and Thread.

Trends affect us all, whether we like it or not. With even the most conservative clothes, the cut of trousers and suit jackets in shops will change in subtle ways from one year to the next. Over a longer timeframe, popular haircuts and styles also change, and in European culture these changes can be dramatic. Be aware that if you are living in a new country for more than a year, an occasional seasonal update may not be an extravagance, and only prudent.

Style and corporate culture

When my team was based in Canary Wharf, our clients were chiefly in the financial services, and we all wore suits: we simply mirrored the norms of the environment we were in. I would always brief the sales team on suitable attire before a client visit. On a client's premises, you want to be a natural fit, and before a visit, I always briefed the sales team on dress.

One time, I was at my first on-site meeting with a new client. The deal had only recently been signed. When I arrived, I saw everyone – even the most senior staff – in jeans, T-shirts, casual clothes. There I was, in a suit. It did not happen again!

Even if jeans and a T-shirt are ideal, they must always be pressed, neat and clean. There was an occasion once when one of my team came into the office wearing a rather furry overcoat. I could picture the scene at his home that morning. He had rolled out of bed, opened the window, and saw that it was an unusually cold day. So, he dug into the furthest reaches of the wardrobe, and found a warming overcoat.

The trouble was, this overcoat had sat crumpled, collecting lint, dust and whatever else, for too long. Years, probably.

"We need to talk," I said. He listened, while I told him what professional dress looked like. The next working day, a Monday, he turned up in a brown suit, popularly worn at Indian weddings, but rarely seen in English offices. He just doesn't get it, I thought.

Getting to grips with culture

"It is trousers, not pants, Dad."

That was my daughter when she was a bit younger, gently telling me off for calling things the 'wrong' thing. If we were in the US, 'pants' would be okay, but the English don't call trousers 'pants.' In England, pants go under the trousers. Or they'll say something is 'pants' when it is second-rate. (Or just a bit rubbish, or ropey, or awful).

To live, work and succeed in a new culture, subtle distinctions like that one matter. Arriving in a new city, I take time to look, see, and really experience it. I want to observe, take things in. Sometimes, in a new and unfamiliar environment, no matter how careful and how conscientious one is, it is possible to make a small misjudgement. In a European city to visit a client, and meet their chief information officer (CIO), I invited him, as I do others, to visit India and see our site there. Clients usually get quite excited at the thought of visiting India, picturing the Taj Mahal and other splendours.

"I don't want to come," he replied, in a voice so cold it could have chilled drinks. Some Europeans are famously direct communicators. I knew, instantly, that I had made a terrible faux pas of some sort. I just did not know what it was. I didn't know where to look, I was so embarrassed!

"Why don't you want to?" I asked.

"I don't like India," he said.

"How about China? We have a site there," I offered.

"I like China," he replied.

I had recovered. It was probably just the long flight that discouraged him, but these things happen, and a small misstep here or there is absolutely forgivable.

Learning a new culture should not feel like a chore. It can be great fun. After a holiday, I was able to tell colleagues about seeing Snowdonia for the first time. A story like this, told with enthusiasm, is enjoyable to relate and to hear.

One evening, my colleagues and I sought out a famed cocktail bar in London. When we got there, a long line stretched from the bar – and they only served one drink.

One healthy expedition, one not so healthy, but they show how learning about a culture means real, practical, and immersive experiences.

When outsourcing, with each office potentially thousands of miles apart, learning about the counterpart's culture is just as important, but how it happens will look different. Listen carefully to understand the preoccupations and popular topics. Some stereotypes are true! The British do talk about the weather a lot. But that doesn't make the distinctions less valid. There should be a mutual intention to learn about and respect the culture.

And it works both ways. For example, a manager based out of India should be aware that Bank Holidays are treated very seriously in the UK. If they were to ask an English colleague to go to a meeting on a Bank Holiday Monday, that colleague is likely to be put out, even upset by it. But his English colleagues also need to make an effort to understand him. Outsourcing is an attractive option for managing costs, but not to the detriment of positive working relationships.

Dining and gifts

Managing relationships with clients will mean exercising discretion when booking restaurants or buying gifts. You may be able to delegate the administration, but you should be in control.

Mores around eating out can vary: my experience is that Americans will go out for a business lunch, but rarely dinner. When overseas or on-site visits, customers may not wish to eat unfamiliar food. For example, when in China with some European clients, I booked a French restaurant, because there the menu would be like what they enjoyed in Europe. Be aware of taste, allergies and preferred choices when booking restaurants.

Get it right, and dining or choosing a gift for a client can be wonderful. One time, I had a lunch booked in Paris with a French client. It was a short, casual lunch, just catching up; but it was the client's birthday and I wanted to present a suitable gift. I was looking around Harrods in Knightsbridge, wondering what to choose. Burberry? Classic designs, from a luxury English manufacturer. I was aware, however, that the French are proud of their heritage. What about something from a French brand? In Paris, I gave the client a Hermès tie.

When I next saw him, it was at one of our sites in India. I noticed he was wearing the tie. We exchanged a nod, and a little smile.

CONCLUSION

Why is it always David and Goliath, and not Goliath and David? The winner gets first place, and all that comes with it: presence, visibility, respect.

Let us remove the spiritual and biblical context for a moment. Why does David win? He didn't wake up one day, and say, "You know what? I'm going to take these stones, and I'm going to whack him." The feat required discipline, precision and perseverance. The ambition was supported by action, and action founded in integrity.

Know what your ambitions are. Consciously discard the unhelpful myths that may surround your profession (we had fun doing this with sales myths in the Introduction) and make a commitment to learning and research. Business changes quickly, so the approach, tools and methods introduced in Chapter 1 may need to be revisited even when a sales strategy – and a good one – is in place, because the broader global climate asserts its presence in unpredictable ways, the Covid-19 pandemic being a pertinent example.

We have talked in detail about sales processes and account management. Maintaining and refining (the 'pruning' concept introduced in Chapter 6) the day-to-day management of prospects and clients requires a big, and continual, investment of your time. While this can be painstaking, it is essential for working towards a healthy client-supplier relationship – the foundation for growing sales and wallet share.

When looking for new clients, hearing "No"' is part of being in a sales environment. I hope I have given a fair representation of some of the challenges a salesperson and businessperson may contend with. Try to be as analytical as possible (staying close to your metrics is one way of doing this), but as important as processes and techniques are, so is the will to be a self-aware leader (Chapter 4). This extends from personal development to conversation, how you dress and even gift-giving. Being self-aware is vital to your long-term success as a businessperson and leader.

Self-awareness also makes for a much richer experience in the workplace and with clients. Seeing your personal progress from month to month and year to year is one of the rewards of hard work. But with all this talk of perseverance and effort, please do not forget to enjoy yourself – take your time in new cities and cultures and appreciate the privilege of being able to visit. In more strenuous phases, 'work' and 'life' can become interchangeable terms, so take care to ensure that work is where you want to be, and that the work is best for you.

I began *The Sales Mindset* talking about strategy, values, and behaviours. I hope that by sharing my experiences it is clear that these things have real, practical application. While your goals may take one, three or 10 years to achieve, the first steps can be taken today. Let's start walking.